How much can I hold?
With Your hand in mine, Jesus,
I can hold the whole world
Since You already have it.
How much can I hold?
Only one handful at a time
Poured out as a gift to those
That share my path.
How much can I hold?
I hold the hem of Your garment
Over Your people
And pray for protection and blessing.
How much can I hold?
I hold nothing except Your hand
Lord of all heaven and earth
For everything belongs to You
My days are in Your hands
And it is I who am held
By You.

A.G.A. Collins

Acknowledgments

Greg Stigter
Sean Quental
Alison Collins
Bryce Percival
Jenny Percival
Chaim Bentorah
Shelagh Ryan
Beck Robinson

Contents

1	*How Much Can I Hold?* A.G.A. Collins
5	Introduction
6	*Capernaum*
8	**The Sun of Righteousness**
54	Notes
63	The Nation of Israel and the Tallit
64	Discussion Questions
66	Prayer
68	Acknowledgments and Attributions
70	*Serenity,* John Greenleaf Whittier

INTERPRETED BY
Love

Introduction

Interpreted by Love is the seventh volume in this series. To think I only ever envisaged one! Appropriately, it signals a change. The change is slight but significant, and is due to my own growth in understanding of the ministry of Jesus as I've written these books.

Of course, this volume still about the healing of history and about the work of Jesus in repairing the brokenness of the past. However, up until now, the specific focus of each story has been on the geography. It's been on the location itself and how it's so important it should influence the way we interpret the meaning of the miracle Jesus performed there. Once we delve into the history of the location we're given, we quickly discover Jesus was never healing a random individual. He always chose someone who was a perfect representative of the harm that particular place had suffered in the past.

This book casts off the constraints of geography and instead begins to look at clues offered by the names within the text. I would have very much liked to continue with the links between geography and history but, unfortunately, most towns in Galilee where Jesus proclaimed His true identity through signs and wonders are not featured in the Hebrew Scriptures. Their backstories are obscured in such deep shadow that we have to look for other evidence to direct us. By using names as a guide, we can begin to glimpse the sutures Jesus applied as He stitched together the wounds of the past. Strange as it may seem, Jesus brought healing to healing – or rather, the arts of healing – and exercised divine healing over human healing. He needed to tackle the source of the problem in the far past as well as the issue in the present.

Now one thing I've learned is this – if Jesus was involved in mending any historical wound, then no matter how many centuries had passed, it was still festering, still seeping, still bleeding. There was no scar because the injury hadn't healed.

There's only one story in this book. It's longer than usual and is written in numerical-literary style. I haven't entirely ignored the geography, because the sole name we are given is, most often, connected with a particular region within Israel. That name pointed me to the geographical clues that showed where to look for the historical damage.

Ultimately, this story connects to the narrative, *Walking the Darkness*, in the fourth book in this series, WHERE HIS FEET PASS. The story starts out with a lot of background so that it's clear what is happening one day in Capernaum when a woman who had been bleeding for twelve years came to Jesus. She, of course, represents a heartbreaking figure in Israel's history. An ancient tragedy forms the backdrop to her life. And that tragedy had been bleeding – not for twelve *years*, but for as many *centuries* and half as much again.

Anne Hamilton
Seventeen Mile Rocks
1 May 2023

But for you who fear My name,
the Sun of Righteousness will rise
with healing in His wings.

Malachi 4:2 NLT

Luke 8:44 ISV

She came up behind Jesus
and touched the tassel of His garment,
and her bleeding stopped at once.

The Sun of Righteousness

This narrative is told from the perspective of a ruler of a synagogue in Capernaum in Galilee.

My father loved telling stories. He was a fine orator who would embellish the tales of ancient heroes with miracles and marvels. So I grew up enthralled by the daring deeds of my namesake, Jair the giant-killer, conqueror of kingdoms, bright and glorious leader of legend whose thirty sons rode thirty donkeys through the thirty cities he had taken, single-handedly.

Oh, perhaps not single-handedly, my father would admit after a dramatic pause — Moses and Joshua had been involved in those battles too. But they had received the majority of the credit while Jair got a solitary line. My father made it his life's work to rectify the imbalance.

So, other boys would play at David with his slingshot bravely preparing to face Goliath and the Philistine army, but I'd always be Jair battling against Og and his ghostly Rephaim warriors. Goliath, my father would point out with a disdainful shrug, certainly deserved his formidable reputation. Nonetheless he was a mere dwarf compared to the monstrous king Og.

I thought for years my father exaggerated, but then one Sabbath, I was actually paying attention to the Torah portion he was reading. To my surprise, it mentioned the size of Og's iron bed.[1] If that was anything to go by, then the last of the Rephaim was almost half as tall again as Goliath.

1. Deuteronomy 3:11

One day, when I was twelve, a significant age in our family, my father asked if I would like to see the cities of Jair and the remains of Og's sun temple. I think he suspected I'd come to disbelieve in the apparent excesses of his stories and wanted me to regain my enthusiasm for our clan history. The excuse for this adventure was a visit to his cousin down in Gadara, one of the cities of the Decapolis.

How can I describe a time that was, at one and the same time, so fearful and so disillusioning? It is beyond telling. What I can speak of is the stories my father told on that journey. There were many, but four in particular stand out in memory for me, four that were part of my heritage, four that belonged to the land that shaped me, four that wonder-beyond-wonder I saw woven together in a marvel and a miracle one day, long years afterwards, in the streets of Capernaum.

My father hired a boat so we could cross the lake to Bethsaida. It was a fine day, the sun dappling the water. We didn't stop at Bethsaida, but hurried through after buying provisions. As we headed for Gamla, the fortress named for the camel's hump of a hill where it was perched, my excitement was high. And it was

not in the least dimmed by the long trudge and the steep climb up the narrow path to the ancient city. We stayed the night in a squalid inn before setting out at dawn into the high wilderness.

My father had bought a tent the previous day. I helped him strap the roll to his back. We stepped out the fortress gate just as the sun hoisted itself onto the horizon. We'd barely reached the far side of the camel's hump when a sharp-edged wind picked up, buffeting us with erratic pulsing shrieks. The sound was an unnerving mix of wailing grief and manic laughter, but I didn't mind. I was too full of joy and enthusiasm to let it affect me — at least at first. It was only the cold I found objectionable.

Several times I saw a heap of rocks in the distance, big enough to shelter us, but as I ran towards them I saw they were doorways to the underworld — two massive stones used as pillars with a slab lintel on top. I would stop, startled but not afraid, reminded that this had once, long ago, been the territory of the Rephaim, the ghost warriors. My admiration for Jair soared — he must have been intensely vigilant to not be surprised by any ambush from one of these doorways to a netherhell.

I soon began to weary of the fist-like punches of wind and began to wonder if Jair's ancient enemies still guarded their upper-world lands against intruders like us. My eyes stung and I kept my head down, trying to keep the bite of the wind from my face. We were heading north-east. It thought it a strange direction but didn't mention it, even when I came to realise my father was always choosing the road less-travelled whenever we came to a junction. Before long, any sign of marked path petered out and we walked across bare, exposed ground until we reached a great edifice of dark stones — a remnant, my father told me, of the work of the giants. The wall must have been at least three times my height. It was clear this was what he had brought me to see.

It was an eerie, desolate place — and, as we approached, the wind dropped and I could hold my head up to see that the stones were not joined together. The wall was a loose construction — a simple wide and high barrier dividing the outside from whatever was inside. However, even I could see it had no defensive value at all. 'What was it used for?' I asked.

'In the old days,' Father explained, 'before the temple in Jerusalem, our people used to gather at gilgals, where we would dance and sing as we circled the sanctuary in the centre. Our gilgals were walled too, but not so high as this, so the people could see the priests at the altar while they were circling around the perimeter and praising God as they went. And another difference is that our gilgals were shaped like the sole of a foot.'[2]

2.
This interpretation of a 'gilgal' comes from the work of archaeologist Adam Zertal, who discovered several massive footprint-shaped structures in the Jordan Valley. He also uncovered an altar, possibly built by Joshua. It is within a temple complex, also built in the shape of a giant footprint, at Mount Ebal in Samaria. 'Gilgal' is therefore to be understood not so much the name of a specific encampment near Jericho, but a term for a worship sanctuary. This includes but is not limited to the one near Jericho. The 'sandal' or 'foot' design seems to be a pattern in keeping with God's promise that Joshua would inherit everywhere he put the sole of his foot.

I couldn't tell from the outside of the wall what form the structure had. 'What's this shaped like, abba?'

'A circle, a wheel. It's about a stadia[3] across from one side to the other. And it is thought it is a similar thing to our gilgals — a place of worship. It was most likely a sun temple.' He pointed to the wall, indicating its size from bottom to top. 'Just short of six cubits, I'd say. So Goliath would have been able to peek over the top.'

'Do you think he was here, abba? I thought he was from Gath, on the south coast.'

My father didn't answer. He was musing to himself, as he gauged the height of the wall. 'Perhaps I was wrong to think the worshippers here would not have been able to see the altar at the centre. They were giants, after all.'

I shivered at that moment, and not with the wind.

'Let's find the entrance,' my father said.

I didn't know what to say. I didn't know if I felt scared or not. I was surprised my father was even thinking of exploring. 'Isn't this an unholy place, abba? Surely it's been used for divination and idolatry and unclean sacrifice and savage ceremonies...' I paused, seeing I wasn't making the slightest impression. 'Why didn't Jair demolish it?'

My father strode along a fair stretch of wall before answering. 'I don't know his reasons.' He sighed. 'But I imagine they were something like David's reasons for not destroying the threshing floor of Araunah but buying it as a site for the temple instead. Araunah was a Canaanite king, you know, and their threshing floors would have been like this wheel — a place to circle around and around, communing with their Baals, performing divination, pronouncing doom, solemnising rituals.'

I'd never heard my father speak like this before. 'But it's the Temple,' I protested.

'That doesn't make its foundation any less defiled.'

'But it's where Abraham was willing to sacrifice Isaac. That must make it...' I hesitated. *Holy? Sanctified? Blessed? Consecrated?*

3. Approximately 158 metres or 172 yards.

'Listen to that story more carefully,' my father suggested. 'It was Moriah, the land of the Amorites, that our forefather went to. If you attend closely, you'll understand the ram was caught in a thicket surrounding a threshing floor. It was natural in Abraham's thinking to choose to build an altar there. Such places were channels for his neighbours to contact their departed kings and ruling divinities. They were portals to the underworld and to high heaven.'

Like this sun temple. I felt uneasy. *But if Abraham could go to a Canaanite sanctuary with the intention of making a sacrifice, then it might not be wrong for us to enter this old temple of Og's.* But then a terrible, terrible thought gripped me. *What if my father was intending to sacrifice me, here in this place?*

'I see you're struggling with the idea that David bought a corrupted site for the Temple,' my father said. 'Surely you remember Ezekiel's words when he was chastising Jerusalem.'

That wasn't what I was struggling with, at all. But, as soon as he spoke, I did remember what Ezekiel said and the answer popped, unbidden, from my tongue. *'Your mother was a Hittite and your father an Amorite.'*[4] It had always seemed a deliberate, almost slanderous provocation to me, but now I realised it was simple truth.

My father clapped with delight. 'You will be like your mother's father — a synagogue leader. I see it now.'

His words comforted me so much I was almost ready to faint. He wouldn't be talking of my future if he had any plans of slaying me right now.

My father clasped my shoulder. 'Despite the Temple's unholy beginnings, there is great hope, my son. Great hope. Isaiah promised us a new and hallowed cornerstone, a sure and precious foundation. The Name, blessed be He, will choose to complete the workmanship Himself and set it in place.'[5]

My thoughts were on a new track. *And if the Lord needs to establish a new foundation, then it follows there's something wrong with the original.* I began to see the line of my father's

4.
Ezekiel 16:45 ESV

5.
Isaiah 28:16

reasoning and, although I was no longer afraid, I felt the first sinking weight of disillusionment.

My father's sigh was deep. 'It's been a long wait. A very long wait. I pray that this new building of Herod's may be the fulfilment of Isaiah's prophecy.' But his voice said that he doubted it.

We had been walking the perimeter of the wall as we talked. 'The doorway!' My father's shout was sudden and triumphant. 'Facing due north. Of course, I should have realised.' He turned around to point to a white shoulder of mountain on the far horizon, visible above a black ridge. 'Hermon of the everlasting snows.' He shook his head. 'The peak where the Watcher angels descended to seek the fairest of women to be their brides. Their children, the giants and the mighty lords of old must have liked to be within sight of the celestial gateway where their fathers first entered this world.'

I focussed on the black ridge that hid much of our view of the snow-capped mountain. Caves — *and are those tombs just there?* — dotted the serpentine curve of the ridge. *Is it a natural formation or a manmade mound?*

My father followed my gaze as it slid from west to east. 'Before Jair conquered Argob, this was Bashan, the serpent's country.'

'Is this Argob?' I asked.

My father laughed and turned back to the doorway. 'Doesn't it look like a heap of stones to you?' He waved his arms towards the walls on either side. 'You know, my son, mighty as Og and his Rephaim were, they were no match for Jair of the thirty sons, thirty donkeys and thirty villages. He subdued this Argob,[6] this land of stone heaps and dolmen tombs, and he gave it as an inheritance to his descendants.'

And so, despite my misgivings, I followed him into the stone wheel and began to walk the concentric circles of its labyrinth. *Because I was Jairus, named for Jair of Gilead, son of Manasseh, son of Joseph, son of Jacob.* And I was brave — brave with the reckless ignorance of a twelve-year-old boy whose dreams had always been of heroes and champions. But brave too with the determined knowledge of a boy old enough to know it is time to face his fears.

So, of course I followed my father in.

I would never do the same with my own children or their children. But I understand now my father's compulsion. Sometimes to recognise Truth, we have to identify the counterfeit first.

So we went around and around between the high walls, in hushed silence, shielded from the wind, warmed by the light of late springtime, until we reached the very centre of Og's sun temple. There, my father reached into his pack and took out his tallit.[7] Wrapping it slowly and reverently around himself, he began to finger the knots of the tzitzit.[8]

6.
'Argob' means *stone heaps*.

7.
A tallit is a prayer shawl. Its corners or ends are called *wings*. When Scripture speaks of sheltering in the shadow of God's wings, the symbolism is not that of a bird, but of a prayer shawl.

8.
The tzitzit attached to a prayer shawl are knotted cords that form the fringe. The cords were fingered by the person as they prayed.

Surely, I thought in disbelief, *he's not going to pray. Not here of all places.* He reached out for my hand and pulled me under the wings of the tallit, close within the curve of his arm. And then he raised the corners of the prayer shawl high and he shouted in a loud voice, *'The Sun of Righteousness will rise with healing in His wings.'*[9]

The howl at that moment was terrifying. My father said later it was just the wind, but I am sure he merely said that to comfort me. It seemed like the battle cry of an entire army and it came, I was sure, from the caves on the serpentine ridge. All the Rephaim, the ghost warriors of the underworld, had heard his cry and were duly enraged — my father's words were a direct challenge not just to their power but to their very identity. But I didn't understand the significance of his words for many years.

At the time, I only knew I had never been so frightened in all my life. Nor have I been since. No, perhaps that's a slight exaggeration. It comes second, but only just, to the moment long afterwards when I realised my daughter was dying and had just minutes to live.

My father lowered the wings of his prayer shawl over me and held me close as he invoked The Name and pronounced blessings on our day and on the land we travelled through. And then we walked back around the labyrinth and left the sun temple. As we journeyed south, through the rest of the day, I kept glancing back at its grey brooding stones and the black serpentine mound beyond it and the white mountain on the far horizon until, one by one, they all disappeared from sight and my heart stopped thudding quite so strenuously.

We stayed overnight in a village so tiny there was no inn. But there was an old woman who welcomed us, even before she knew we had bread and salted fish to share. 'There are still some places where the traditions of hospitality are kept,' my father said the following day as we headed for Chaspho. He wanted to reach the Roman road there that would give us an easy highway to follow.

9.
Malachi 4:2 NLT

We walked for two days, spending the nights in our tiny, cosy tent. On the third day, our morning was interrupted once again by another monument in the landscape. This one was not frightening at all. It was simply a cairn of stones. My father picked up one from the ground as we approached it and gestured to me to do the same. We placed our rocks on the already-substantial pile.

And then we sat on the tent-roll while father took out his tallit once more and fingered the tzitzit as he prayed.

'What is this place?' I asked when he had finished and brought out the waterskin and some dried figs. And so began the second of the stories that my father told on that journey that had such great bearing on my future.

'This is the place that Laban named "Jegar Sahadutha" and that Jacob called "Galeed" when they met.'[10]

'Witness heap,' I said.

My father nodded. 'Now Uncle Laban, you will remember, had out-tricked the trickster, his nephew Jacob, and had got him to work for more than twenty years for a wife he didn't want, as well

10.
Genesis 31:47

as a wife he did want, plus some speckled and striped sheep and goats. And finally, when Jacob had had enough of his uncle's deceptions...'

'You forgot to mention the unspeckled sheep and unstriped goats,' I said.

'Indeed, that was very remiss of me,' my father admitted. 'Still when Jacob had had enough of his uncle's deceptions, he left the land of Aram to return to his own country. He did not tell Laban he was going with his wives and his daughter, his flocks and his eleven sons. For Benjamin, *the son of the south*,[11] the only child born in Jacob's own country, had not yet come from his mother's womb. Jacob left secretly. However he told his wives to pack up and get ready and so, unbeknownst to him, Rachel, his beloved, his favourite, stole the figurines of the teraphim belonging to her father.'

'I don't understand teraphim, abba. Sometimes they seem like idols, and sometimes like ghosts and sometimes like little guards that watch over entrances.'

'They are quite hard to explain. The teraphim were not principalities or fallen angelic lords like the Watchers. They were the housing for the spirits of dead ancestors. So they would have

11.
Benjamin is usually translated *son of my right hand,* however it can also be rendered *son of the south.*

been Laban's way of consulting his deceased forbears for their guidance in prosperity and healing. They would be like personal Rephaim, *spirit-healers*. The figures of the teraphim serve as a channel to contact their departed souls. They were an inheritance that should have gone to Laban's sons.'

'So it was here in the land of the Rephaim that he was angry about the loss of his own private Rephaim.' It seemed to fit. The Rephaim of the land would have emboldened his anger when he caught up to Jacob. A curious thought occurred to me. 'Jacob never told Laban about The Name, did he?'

My father shook his head. 'It is a strange shadow in our nature that our people can never bear to share the knowledge of The Name, blessed be He, with the Arameans who, after all, are our relatives. You are right. Jacob did not share that ultimate blessing with Laban.' He raised a finger to draw my attention. 'But think, my son. Did Elisha share with Naaman, the commander of Aram's armies who came to him to be healed of leprosy? Naaman was open to learning but did Elisha take the opportunity? And did he share with Hazael, who came to him seeking the word of the Lord? Remember that Elijah had been told by The Name to anoint Hazael as king of Aram, but he did not. Nor did Elisha. Imagine how many wars might have been avoided had the Arameans come to a knowledge of The Name.'

A spark of inspiration ignited in my soul. '*We* could teach the *Romans!*'

My father's smile fed the flame in me. 'So when you become synagogue leader, you will allow centurions and auxiliaries from the local station into Sabbath services?'

I was instantly deflated, thinking of the bitter controversy that would ensue. 'There must be some way,' I said, scowling.

My father's eyes twinkled as he handed me another dried fig. 'I'm sure you'll work it out.' He gazed at the cairn. 'This is *witness heap*,' he said, 'in whatever language you choose.[12] And I speak to it and I say, "In the name of the Fear of Isaac and the God of Abraham, we agree with the pledge between Laban and Jacob.

12.
Genesis 31:47

The Lord watching over us, we will always treat our wives and our daughters with honour." Is that not so, Jairus?'

I came out of my stupor of thinking.

'Amen!' I pronounced belatedly.

Then I frowned. 'But, abba, what if the dishonour is accidental? Like when Jacob cursed Rachel, not intentionally, but because he wasn't to know that she had stolen the teraphim when he said to Laban that whoever had taken them should not live. And she died not long after. So was that Jacob's fault?'

'Was that his fault? I think it depends largely on why he said it. Why do you think Jacob uttered such a curse?'

I thought about Rachel sitting on the teraphim hidden under the camel's saddle and tricking her father by explaining she couldn't get up because she was in the bleeding period of her menstrual cycle. It was a lie, because Benjamin must have been present in her womb even then. More than a lie, it was dishonour of her father. And more than dishonour of her father, it was an insult to her ancestors to sit on their statues. It was a foolish thing Jacob said, since he didn't know who the thief was. After all, it could even have been his favourite son, Joseph. What then?

'Maybe he thought Laban was trying to swindle him again,' I said finally.

'Perhaps. But it was a very unwise risk, don't you think? Unless he suspected the wrong person of taking them and wanted to be rid of her.'

Her? I leaned against my father for support. I wished he'd open up his prayer shawl again and hide me in the shadow of its wings. 'Leah?' I asked in a very small voice.

'If he did suspect her, and she would be the logical choice since she was the elder and the most likely to covet the teraphim, he had the perfect opportunity to be rid of her. He didn't care for her, after all, or her sons. When Simeon was imprisoned in Egypt, what did he say? That he couldn't risk Benjamin's life to try to save him, because Benjamin was the only son he had left. It was as if the others didn't exist.' My father shrugged. 'I'm sure he thought that Laban would never kill Leah but, if they found the teraphim in her belongings, it would be the perfect excuse to send her — and her maidservant — away in one go. A simple solution to solving the domestic harmony problem.'

I didn't like to think there was malice in Jacob's manipulations. I'd always seen him as seeking the shrewd advantage, not as full of black-hearted cunning. 'He must have known eventually it was Rachel,' I said. 'Perhaps when he told his wives to bury all their figurines of foreign gods[13] under the tree at Shechem he was trying to save her.'

My father nodded. 'Wise as it is to always honour your wife and your daughters, it is wiser still not to dishonour the lords of calamity.[14] Remember *The Testament of Moses* where it says that even the archangel Michael, when he was arguing with the devil over the body of Moses, took care not to dishonour his enemy but simply said, "The Lord rebuke you!"[15] If ever you encounter a demon, that is the best approach. There are those who say that you should strive to learn the demon's name in order to have authority over it, and therefore the power to cast it out, but it is better to focus on the Lord's Name, not the name of the demon.'

'Have you ever encountered a demon, abba?'

13.
Genesis 35:4

14.
The word for *foreign* in the description of the idols that Jacob instructed his wives to bury is derived from the word for *calamity*.

15.
This interaction between the devil and Michael is quoted in Jude 1:9. Origen attributed it to *The Testament of Moses*, also called *The Assumption of Moses*. Jude uses it to bolster his argument that believers should not dishonour, revile, insult or slander any spirits, even the satan. He then goes on to detail the fearful consequences of such behaviour.

My father put his arm around me. 'Do you think I would have brought you through such dangerous country if I did not know how to call on the Name of the Lord and ask Him to rebuke the Rephaim?'

I blinked. I swallowed. So there were Rephaim all around us. Probably Rephaim following us. *But abba is not afraid. He truly believes in the protection of The Name.* So I took courage. I took a deep breath and I caught my father's eye. He laughed. And then I laughed. Because at last I understood that Jair of the thirty sons, and thirty donkeys and thirty villages did not deserve his fame because he was a giant-killer but because he put his trust in The Name to defend both him and his children in this land where nearly every rock pile was a doorway to the underworld.

He had found protection under the wings of the Lord's prayer shawl. David, too, had found that secret refuge. *'Hide me in the shadow of your wings,'* he'd sung, *'from the wicked who are out to destroy me, from my mortal enemies who surround me.'*[16]

My father stood up and reached out his hand. And then he pulled me, once more into the shelter of his tallit, and I knew I had understood his message. Many years later I was to discover that he thought there were just as many demons in Capernaum as there were in the rocky wilderness of Gilead — and, by that time, I was prepared to believe he was right.

My father folded up his prayer shawl and tucked it away, and we set off south once more.

We came to Raphana, *the place of healing*, where my father told his shortest story.

'Why are the Rephaim named for *healing?*' I asked him.

'Because, unlike The Name, they are liars, tricksters and thieves.'

It was unfortunate that his words made me think of Jacob and, although I tried to elicit more information from him, he would not be drawn. Finally I asked, 'Is it dishonouring to call them liars, tricksters and thieves, abba?'

16.
Psalm 17:8 NIV

'An interesting point, my thoughtful son. It is good to see you have taken my words to heart, even when I have missed the mark. Very well, I amend my words in case they may be construed as dishonour. I ask the Lord's forgiveness for speaking ill of His creation, fallen though it is. But this I say to those who desire for themselves the honour due only to Him: there is but one healer, Yahweh Rapha. There is no other. From Him comes all power and might for the mending of the body, from Him comes all knowledge of plants for medicine and minerals for cures, from Him comes all miracles of healing, be they swift or slow.'

We spent three days in Gadara with my father's cousin. There was some question of an old inheritance to be resolved — land, it seemed, that no one really wanted. My father had first right of redemption but it was desolate country, too far from Capernaum to be of use to us. He was willing to forgo his rights if the cousin was prepared to try to cultivate it. Myrrh trees was what he suggested. I could see he had given it much thought because such trees would do well in such a barren landscape though it would be many years before they could be cut for balm.

Once the cousin accepted, my father took off his sandal and passed it over.[17] 'We can formalise it the new way, too, if you like, Mordecai,' he said, 'with a sealed scroll.'

17. Ruth 4:7

Mordecai took the sandal. 'This is enough,' he said.

I could see he and my father genuinely liked each other. Both of them knew much of the old lore that had been forgotten since the Greeks and Romans had taken over. It wasn't Babylon that buried our stories, it was Macedon. My father, however, seemed to be intent on reviving them. Or at least ensuring that they were passed on to me, as the next generation.

We went back, praise be to The Name, by way of the Jordan. And as we came to it, travelling down through the Decapolis and then by the Brook Cherith where Elijah had been fed by ravens, my father told his longest and most important story. The one that I would need thirty years in the future, to make sense of all that happened in that moment when the Rephaim came for my daughter and would not be denied.

We were still in Gilead. It was not yet the rainy season so we were able to walk the dry bed of the Cherith. From time to time we would scamper up the banks and pick ripe carob pods on the locust trees. Once we raided a wild bees' hive. And just before we reached the Jordan, my father spotted a walkway up the cliff. He must have been looking out for it because it was nearly hidden by thick undergrowth.

So we climbed up to a ruined city with a stunning view straight across the river to the temples of Scythopolis. Their high white pillars were dazzling, even under a sullen sky. Dionysius and Herakles, these were the deities worshipped by the descendants of the Scythians who had rebuilt the city centuries ago.

We sat under an ancient terebinth tree that was, I realised later, more likely than not the place where the bones of Saul and Jonathan were buried[18] before David had them reinterred outside Jerusalem. My father handed me the waterskin to sip.

'Jairus,' he began, 'we will soon ford the river. People on the other side think differently from those on this side.'

'Like Judeans think differently from Galileans?'

'More so.' My father pointed across to the walls and gates of the bright city on the far side of the Jordan. 'That was once the Philistine fortress of Beth Shan.' He turned to the tumbledown remains behind us. 'And this was once the proud city of Jabesh Gilead. It was destroyed because its citizens did not respond to the call to war sent out during the days of the Judges.'

I remembered the story. It was brutal and tragic. Almost all the clans of Benjamin had been exterminated in the war. There were only six hundred men who survived. So, because they hadn't meant to destroy all of their brothers in Benjamin, the men of the tribes of Israel decided to attack the one city that had not

18.
1 Chronicles 10:12

participated in the war. They then killed everyone there except for the young unmarried maidens and they handed them over as trophies of war to the survivors of Benjamin so they could rebuild their tribe.[19]

'Now not long after the destruction of Jabesh Gilead,' my father said, 'before it was rebuilt, another call to war went out.[20] You'd think the tribes of Israel would have learned their lesson from the example here, but it was not so. Now the Ammonites were attacking the towns here in Gilead and the situation was desperate. So desperate that the elders and civic leaders swallowed their pride and sent for the chief of an outlaw band who'd been exiled by his family. Jephthah was the son of a prostitute and his brothers didn't want him to inherit. So they'd banished him and he'd wound up in the land of Tob. A small, tough band of other outcasts gathered around him.'

This was another story my father had told before. This time, however, I was reminded of David, in the days when Saul was hunting him. David, too, had gathered a loyal band of mighty men around him.

'Now Jephthah wasn't sure the elders' promises to him would be kept. But, after getting them to repeat their assurances in the presence of the Lord, he was convinced they would keep their word to make him their commander. So he sent a diplomatic message to the king of the Ammonites. To cut a long message short and the story shorter, the king sneered. So Jephthah sent out a call to war around all the tribes and raised a mighty army. He stormed through Gilead and devastated twenty Ammonite towns.'

'Twenty?' I said. 'Jair took thirty.'

'Jair had all of Israel to support him,' my father said. 'Jephthah did not.' He sighed and pulled the tallit from his pack. 'The people of Ephraim, our closest kin in the tribal brotherhood, the very people who'd been party to the destruction of Jabesh Gilead just a few years previously, they were the ones who deliberately stayed away.'

'And then,' I said, 'they lied about it.'

19.
Judges 19–21

20.
It is easy to get the impression that the book of Judges is arranged entirely in chronological order. Most of it is. However the last and longest tale that climaxes in a civil war, but starts with the theft of silver by a man called Micah and his subsequent employment of a Levite as his personal household priest, occurs in the days when Phinehas, grandson of Aaron, was the high priest. That dates it to the earliest period of the Judges. Therefore the story of Jephthah and the Ephraimites occurs after that conflict.

He trains my hands for battle; my arms can bend a bow of bronze.

Psalm 18:34 NIV

My father nodded. 'The people of Ephraim and some of the people of Manasseh, too, particularly the half-tribe from the other side of the Jordan, look down on those who come from Gilead. They think the clans from over here in the east are inferior in some way. No doubt their attitude was made worse by Jephthah's mother.'

'That's no excuse to ignore a call to war.'

My father nodded. 'Now, of course, when Jephthah was so spectacularly victorious, the leaders of Ephraim began to be more than a little worried. They'd ignored his call to war. What if he turned on them in the same way as they'd turned on Jabesh Gilead? So, deciding that the best defence is a good offence, they massed their army and crossed the border.'

Unfolding his tallit and pulling it around him, my father pointed to the fords far below us. 'There are two places that the men of Ephraim could have forded the Jordan. One is down near Jericho, the other is here, opposite Beth Shan.'

I flicked a glance over my shoulder at the ruins of Jabesh Gilead. *They should have got the warning. Or perhaps the warning made them more determined.*

I could see my father following my gaze. 'They marched up to Jephthah's home,' he said, 'and they announced, "We're offended! You had a war and you didn't invite us. We're going to burn your house down with you in it."

'It doesn't work very well as an apology,' I commented.

'It's not very humble either,' my father said with a shake of his head. 'Now Jephthah was in no mood for diplomacy. His daughter — she was unmarried, so she would have been just about your age — was roaming the hills of Gilead, in the middle of two months of mourning because Jephthah had made a rash vow to sacrifice the first thing out of his door if the Lord granted him victory against the Ammonites.'[21]

I didn't like that part of the story, so I interrupted, 'He growled at the men of Ephraim that they were trying to blame him, when they were the ones who'd ignored the call to war. Then Jephthah summoned his own men to attacked the intruders. But they turned and ran all the way back to the Jordan.'[22]

'Who's telling this story?'

I dropped my head, abashed.

'Go on,' my father said. 'You were doing well.'

I looked up and he was smiling.

'Well,' I said watching his reaction closely, 'some of Jephthah's men had got to the fords first. And when one of the raiders came up to them, they'd ask, "Are you from Ephraim?" and if the man said, "No," then Jephthah's men would smile and politely request...' I paused, wanting to make sure I got the words the right way around. 'Please say "Shibboleth."' I made it a long, exaggerated sibilant sound and my father said nothing. I was relieved. That meant I'd got it correct. 'But if the man said, "Sibboleth," then he was executed.'[23]

My father was watching me watching him. 'And what is the difference between "Shibboleth" and "Sibboleth"?' he asked.

There was a twinkle in his eye, so I was concerned once more. I was about to say, 'Accent,' but I thought twice and decided not to. 'They both mean *an ear of grain*,' I said, sounding less doubtful than I suddenly felt.

21.
Judges 11:30–31

22.
There was a forest known as the Forest of Ephraim just south of the Brook Cherith, between what is now the Wadi el-Yabis (also known as the Wadi el-Rayyan) and the gorge of the Jabbok River. It is possible this forest was named for the area where the men of Ephraim fled as they made their way to the Jordan. It was in this forest, during the time of king David, that his rebel son Absalom was killed after his thick, luxuriant hair was caught in the branches of a tree and he could not free himself.

23.
Judges 12:5–6

My father took my hand and, opening it, laid the tzitzit of his prayer shawl across my palm. The knots in the fringe felt like the seeds in an ear of grain. He didn't say anything.

I broke the silence finally. 'Don't they?'

'Yes, they do,' my father said. 'An ear of grain.' He ran his finger over the tzitzit in my palm. 'But they come from different sources. "Shibboleth" comes from the word for a flowing stream, the train of a robe, the hem of a garment, the fringe of a shawl. "Sibboleth" comes from a word for carrying a heavy burden.' He stroked the tzitzit again, tickling my palm. His sigh was heavy. 'Remember that I said that people on this side of the Jordan think differently from those on the other side?'

I nodded. I couldn't speak. The moment was too solemn. And I didn't know why.

'The people of Gilead and Peraea,' he said, 'not the newcomers of the Decapolis, but the people of Israel who trace their lineage back to Gad, Manasseh and Reuben lived alongside the Ammonites and Arameans for centuries. There wasn't always war. And in the times of peace, we learned some of their ways. We make covenant with blood and salt. They make vows of covenant loyalty to one another by stooping to hold the hem of another's garment.'[24]

24. See https://torahresource.com/hem-covenant-sign/

It took me a full minute of thinking, all the while feeling as if the feather-light tzitzit on my palm was becoming intolerably heavy, to work it out. 'It wasn't a test of accent at all. The men of Gilead offered the invaders from Ephraim a way of escape from the terrible bind they'd created. To say "shibboleth" was to say, "I am willing to renew the age-old covenant between the clans." But to say, "sibboleth" is to refuse that chance. It says we are not equals; you are our inferiors, our servants; get a move on, you slaves, and carry us across the river.'

My father folded my palm over the tzitzit. 'And that's why forty-two thousand warriors of Ephraim were killed. Because they would rather have died than lose their status in Israel.' He hugged me tight. 'Never forget, Jairus, when you see that kind of pride it is not courage. It is diabolical in origin and divides brother from brother down countless generations. Twelve hundred years and more since the massacre at the Jordan — and the wound is not yet healed.'

'Then it never can be,' I said, swamped by a sense of quiet despair.

'Of course it can!' My father stood up, pulling me with him. Raising the wings of his prayer shawl high, he shouted just as he had in Og's temple, *'The Sun of Righteousness will rise with healing in His wings.'*

And then he gathered our belongings and we descended the cliff, forded the Jordan and made our way home. And immersed in a new excitement—that of preparing for my bar mitzvah, I was to forget his expression of faith for another thirty years.

The decades rolled by, busy with… well, busyness. Just everyday busyness. In time, as my father had predicted, I came to be the leader of the synagogue. The position sounds prestigious but, actually, there wasn't a synagogue building, just a rented hall much too small for our needs. Most of my role was taken up dealing with disputes between neighbours or complaints about the examinations for bar mitzvah getting more slip-shod as time went by.

When Jesus had again crossed over by boat to the other side of the lake, a large crowd gathered around Him while He was by the lake.

Mark 5:21 NIV

I had married, I had a wife who was the beloved of my life and a daughter who was my heart's treasure. My father was still alive, he was old and full of years and, although his body was frail, his faith was invincible. 'I shall not die,' he told me one day, 'until I have seen the Messiah who speaks the language of both sides.'

When I asked him what he meant, he said that The Name, blessed be He, had assured him that the Sun of Righteousness would not forget Gilead and Gergesa, Gerasa and Gadara but would walk the lands there, east of the Jordan, to make them whole too. *But for sure He'll be based in Judea,* I thought. 'But will He ever come to Galilee?' I asked.

My father smiled. Then he laughed and laughed. But he would not answer.

One day he presented me with a problem — one much larger than the bar mitzvah tests and the disputes between neighbours. 'Jairus,' he said. 'About the Romans.'

'What about the Romans?' *Has there been a fight I know nothing about?* I'd worked so hard to have good relations between the local garrison and the people of the town. In all of Galilee, we'd become renowned for our peaceful atmosphere and lack of civic unrest.

'Remember, many years ago, you said you'd like to teach the Romans about The Name...'

Appalled, I interrupted him. 'Never!' When had I ever espoused such a naïve and dangerous notion? I couldn't believe my father would suggest I'd strayed so far from the safe orthodoxy of the elders.

'It was a very long time ago,' my father insisted. 'The thing is, there's a soldier who wants to learn...'

'We can't let him.' I couldn't believe how rudely and loudly I was interrupting but everything he was saying was shocking.

'...and you need to figure out how it can be done.' And then he left.

It was a horrifying situation. I couldn't afford to offend the Romans. But I couldn't afford to offend the people of Capernaum, especially those loyal and faithful to The Name. My mind was in a

stew for three whole days. I didn't sleep. I didn't eat. And perhaps because I was so exhausted and was trying to stop myself from being snappish when I was walking down by the lakeside and a fisherman's daughter brought me a fish to bless because the overnight catch was obviously insufficient — 'I'm not a rabbi,' I told her far too sharply — that I saw the solution so suddenly and clearly it was almost a vision.

A hall. *A new hall.* A new hall big enough to have an area exclusively reserved for Gentiles. A hall that needs security, like the Temple in Jerusalem with its Temple Guards. Except, of course, in Capernaum we don't have the luxury of our own security force and we'd never get permission for one. So we only have the Roman auxiliaries. Who, if we could persuade — oh, terrifying thought, *pay?* — them to come, would just happen to hear our teaching while standing on guard. But why not? What did we have to hide?

There was a hall, in the last stages of construction, that might just fit our needs. But it was far beyond our ability to finance, particularly if we were going to pay soldiers to pretend to guard it. But the beauty of that arrangement would be that we could communicate to them what sacrilege meant to us so maybe we could really help defuse the kind of tension that had just occurred in Jerusalem with the imperial standards brought in by Pontius Pilate.

I hurried to the building. And I was somehow not surprised, as I stepped inside, to see my father already there. He was deep in conversation with a young carpenter, whose voice echoed through the building like the sound of many waters. 'It's no longer for rent,' he was saying, 'it is for sale. The owner's circumstances have changed.' He was showing my father a wide stone staircase to the gallery.

Perfect, I thought, as I watched the young man help my father mount the steps in his slow, feeble way. *Perfect for the women and children.* As I looked on the ground floor, I could see a railing of half-columns around three sides, forming an outer court. *It's ideal. The Romans could stand outside the rail. We could put up curtains, not heavy ones like those in the Temple, but sheer ones.* I was trying to think how I would explain why the curtains needed to be sheer to the elders. *First, because we have nothing to hide and, second, because we need to see them as much as they need to see us. We don't want to be taken by surprise.*

The money angle was, however, hopeless. Rent — barely. Buy — impossible. Yet the more I looked, the more I knew this hall had been destined for our community, both Jew and Gentile. There was a podium at the back of the hall, designed for a teacher. On it was an ornately carved seat with a high back and sides. When I went to examine the chair, I realised the seat could be adjusted to different heights. If it were raised and a door mounted in front of it, it would be just right as a shelf to house our scrolls of the Torah, the Prophets and the Writings.

But the money — *unattainable.*

My father and the young carpenter were descending the gallery stairs. I could see that my father found it much easier to come down than go up. He was laughing and a joyful youthfulness had entered his face. It was only later I realised it had entered his walk as well.

'I will speak to my abba.' The carpenter's hand was on my father's shoulder. 'He will arrange matters for you.' He turned to me, his

smile dazzling. 'You want the seat moved up so it is a shelf, and a door on the front?'

Had I been that obvious? 'Oh, I can't ask you to alter anything,' I demurred. 'We don't have the money to buy this.'

'As I said to your abba, I will speak to my abba, and all will be well.' His voice was no longer like the rippling sound of many waters, but like a quiet, distant thunder.

'Please don't do anything without proper authorisation,' I said, suddenly aware of the man's intentions.

'Oh, I never do,' he said.

But I thought by his manner that he considered the matter settled.

My father took my arm. 'Come, come, Jairus, we must go to the garrison.'

I went out the door, preparing to argue with my father in private. That was the last time I saw the carpenter for nearly three years. I heard about him — many times — but, without seeing him, I did not realise I had just met Jesus of Nazareth.

We'd barely stepped out of the hall when a soldier from the local auxiliary station met us. 'I have been directed by the centurion to instruct you to come to the tax booths and sort out the synagogue's finances.' His voice was loud and brash.

Taxes? My heart sank, not just at the prospect of handing more money to the Romans, but at the public embarrassment involved.

'How splendid!' my father exclaimed.

I wondered if he'd slipped into senility, all unnoticed by me. We went down by the fishermen's wharves to the tax booths and there, grim and unsmiling, was Antonius. He and I knew each other from endless representations I'd made to the auxiliaries. The substance of the majority of them was: *pleasepleaseplease, do not ask a Jewish man to carry a pack for a mile on the Sabbath. Any other day, not the Sabbath.*

My negotiations had been about as effective as Julius Caesar's infamous attempt to stop the storm.[25]

Antonius ushered us into a private room and asked us to sit. My stomach felt as if it had dropped to my toes. I'd never been asked to sit in his presence. 'There's been an anomaly with the taxes.' He went to the far side of a table and leaned across it, towering over us. 'So, you understand, we're going to have to keep a closer eye on who is and isn't paying their rightful dues. We therefore need an accurate head count. The simplest way to do this would be to station some men in the outer court of the new synagogue...' He

25.
See: *Like Wildflowers, Suddenly: Jesus and the Healing of History #01*, the first volume in this series.

smiled abruptly. '...and this would have to happen every Sabbath because, of course, the population in a town like this is so fluid.'

I stared. And at some point I realised my jaw must have dropped open because I found I had to close it at the end of his speech. *Oh, King of the Universe, it's Antonius wants to learn about You.* I gulped. *How do I tell him we aren't getting a new synagogue? Come to think of it, how does he know I was thinking of it?* I hadn't even told the town elders yet.

Antonius reached below the table, pulled out a bulging pouch and dumped it in front of us. 'This should sort out the present irregularity in finances but we're going to have to keep a close eye on the matter from now on.'

I was so frozen I was glad my father had the presence of mind to take it and thank him. And then, somehow, we were outside in the sunshine. I was so confused I couldn't think straight. The world had swivelled upside down. A centurion had just paid for our synagogue. And had offered me the perfect excuse to present to the town elders as to why there had to be a Roman presence in it from now on. It was incomprehensible.

'You knew all along it was Antonius who wanted to learn about The Name,' I accused my father.

He nodded. 'The reason he had a violent reputation before he got here was that he doesn't get on with hypocrites. He hasn't mellowed; he's simply been checking you out for years. He's been waiting for the bribe that never came. It seems you've earned his trust. Apparently you explained tithing to him once. So I believe the bag contains tithes from several years of taxes.'

We bought the synagogue outright. It took about three months for the people to get used to the guards in the foyer and outer court, and soon afterwards they even began greeting some of them by name. And, eventually, when word got around — as it inevitably did — how we'd paid for the synagogue, the complaints were far less ferocious than I anticipated. In fact, one of the town elders stopped all the grumbles with the comment: 'The enemy has paid to build a house of worship. Shall we not doubly rejoice?'

Antonius, as it turned out, was absolutely meticulous in checking people out. You'd earn his undying enmity for any attempt at deception, but his quiet and generous protection if you proved your integrity. So I was surprised by his inaction when jostling crowds began to flood through our town, following Jesus of Nazareth around.

Jesus was an itinerant rabbi who often passed through Capernaum and who was beginning to make a name for himself as a miracle-worker. Word had come down from his hometown to watch out for him because he was a blasphemer. Then, to my horror, I received messages from Jerusalem that his healings were done by the power of Beelzebub.[26]

My father, to my deep distress, began to believe he was the Messiah. I could not. Implacably could not, because of all that I was hearing from Judea. Jesus was friends with sinners — surely that lent credence to his power being demonic in origin.

But then Antonius, of all people, caused me to change. Not to belief, no, not that far. But towards neutrality. That, I came to realise, was Antonius' default position while collecting facts, not opinions or biases.

It happened that Antonius had a young servant who was very dear to him. One day the child[27] became paralysed, suffering from an agonising illness. So Antonius, on realising the doctors he had summoned were helpless, went to the gate of Capernaum

26.
Matthew 12:24–28

27.
The Greek word for *servant* indicates he was a child.

with some of the town elders and waited for Jesus to arrive. He explained the situation, and the elders spoke for him, telling Jesus he'd contributed to the building of the synagogue.[28] Jesus immediately offered to come and heal his servant.

Antonius must have already planned very carefully what to say, knowing how much Jesus' reputation would suffer if he went into a Roman house. *'Lord,'* he said — not *rabbi* but *lord* — *'I am not worthy to have you come into my home. Just say the word from where you are, and my servant will be healed. I know this because I am under the authority of my superior officers, and I have authority over my soldiers. I only need to say, "Go," and they go, or "Come," and they come. And if I say to my slaves, "Do this," they do it.'*[29]

Jesus, I was told, was seriously impressed. 'I tell you the truth, I haven't seen faith like this in all Israel! And I tell you this, that many Gentiles will come from all over the world — from east and west — and sit down with Abraham, Isaac, and Jacob at the feast in the Kingdom of Heaven. But many Israelites — those for whom the Kingdom was prepared — will be thrown into outer darkness, where there will be weeping and gnashing of teeth.'[30] Then he told Antonius to go home and it would happen as he had believed. And so it was. And the whole town knew about it.

28. Luke 7:4–5

29. Matthew 8:8–9 NLT

30. Matthew 8:10–12 NLT

After that, I thought about what my father had said The Name had promised him: a Messiah who spoke the language of both sides, who understood the dialect and the culture of the people beyond the Jordan as well as those on this side. And I began to wonder if my father had actually limited the Messiah — what if He spoke all languages and understood all cultures, even that of the Romans?

But because it was imprudent to publicly commit myself, I kept my own counsel and tried to stay above the escalating controversy. I didn't join the crowds that followed Jesus but I did listen to what others said about him. It was so mixed. And then, the day of decision came.

As it always does.

In the year after the healing of Antonius' servant, my own daughter became ill. She was just twelve, the apple of my eye. We were starting to look around for a suitable husband to begin the process of betrothal. I was seriously thinking of involving Antonius in the selection. Would it be unrighteous to ask him to do one of his meticulous checks on the candidate I had in mind?

One morning, my daughter became feverish. My wife thought it was more serious than I did. More to allay her anxiety than anything else, I brought in a doctor. When he came out of the child's room, I could see he was lying as he assured me she'd recover with a tincture he'd sold my wife. I sent immediately for another doctor who was less comforting in his diagnosis. The fever had built by the time he had got there and sometimes my little one screamed in terror and thrashed about on the bed.

The sound tore away thirty years of forgetfulness, shredding it in a single moment. I'd heard that howling shriek before — in the high wilderness, at Og's sun temple, east of the Jordan. The Rephaim had come. They had found me at last and were seeking vengeance.

No, my heart said. *It's not that they have found you, it's that they are always here. Vengeance does not come into it, simply opportunity.*

But still I sensed their desire for my daughter, my treasure, and I did not know what to do. My father came to sit by her bedside. He wrapped himself in his tallit and fingered the tzitzit as he prayed through the night for her healing. A healing that opposed the self-proclaimed healers, the Rephaim, who cure by shrouding their patients in the pall of the underworld.

The morning came and, when I touched her brow, she was on fire. I left as another doctor came in, advising my wife about cool cloths and hot poultices.

And as I strode, unthinking, to the gate, there was Antonius, lounging against a pillar as if he had nothing better to do with his day than wait for my appearance. 'His boat is just coming in to the shore.' He stared at me. 'If you do not go, you will always regret that you did not take a chance for her.' His stare intensified. *'Always.'*

I ran. I brushed past him and hurtled down to the lakeside. A crowd had already gathered but I pushed through them and found myself face to face with the young carpenter who'd fixed the Ark in our synagogue.

Sometimes to recognise Truth, we have to identify the counterfeit first. I'd seen the false healers, so now I knew the true and the real when I saw him. 'Please come,' I begged, throwing myself at his feet, 'my daughter is dying.'

He bent over and whispered, 'I will ask my abba and all will be well.' His voice was still like the sound of many waters, and like the quiet rumbling of distant thunder. And in that moment, I knew it had been no accident that Antonius had financed our synagogue. This carpenter had asked his abba to arrange it, and so it was done. Antonius knew what it was to be under authority, so he did not question his orders.

I scrambled up. My breathing was ragged, my limbs were trembling, as I pushed through the crush of people to allow him to follow me. We had just reached the end of the wharf when he stopped. *'Who touched me?'* he asked.[31] He glanced around, searching eyes with a probing look.

Confronted with that gaze, people began step back as they denied it. A space formed around Jesus. One of his disciples said, *'Master, people are crowding all around and pushing you from every side.'*[32]

'Someone touched me,' he insisted. *'I felt power going out from me.'*[33]

A woman, head bowed, bent almost double, came around from behind him and fell at his feet. I could feel myself become frantic with the urgency of my daughter's need as he raised the woman up and asked for her story. It seemed to me far longer a tale than it really was, as if it would never end. She had been bleeding for twelve years — *twelve*, I thought, *all the years my daughter has been alive* — and she had spent all her money on healers but had not been cured. She only become worse.

Healers, I thought bitterly and distractedly. *Did it matter if the doctors and the Rephaim were in conflict or in an alliance? Only Yahweh Rapha can heal.* And I wondered what I was doing there. Because it didn't matter how much of a wonder-worker this carpenter-rabbi from Nazareth was, only Yahweh Rapha can heal.

31. Luke 8:45 CEV

32. Luke 8:45 CEV

33. Luke 8:46 CEV

The woman spoke on. She'd heard Jesus was coming back from the east of the Jordan, so she thought to herself that if only she touched the hem of his garment, she would be healed. I knew in that moment she'd come herself from Gilead or Peraea because she had the covenant thinking of those places. She didn't say that, of course, but I long remembered what my father had said, 'We make covenant in blood and salt. They make vows of covenant loyalty to one another by stooping to hold the hem of another's garment.'

I'd found out more about the symbolism of this covenant since the day, long ago, when my father had told me of it. Taking the hem of a garment was also a way of proclaiming allegiance to a king. I was sure, as I looked at the shining eyes of the woman, glistening with tears of relief and joy, that she'd intended exactly that. She'd taken hold of the tzitzit of his tallit, the knotted fringe of his prayer shawl, so she would be in unified oneness with the prayers of the Messiah. And not just with his prayers, but with *him* — as her lord.

I'd missed my chance. I wanted to bend now, to kiss the tzitzit, but it would be such an obvious act of desperation. My pride held me back. And then my father's voice exploded into my mind out of a hidden memory: 'Never forget, Jairus, when you see that kind of pride it is not courage. It is diabolical in origin

and divides brother from brother...' Was my pride dividing me from the Messiah?

Jesus touched the woman lightly on the brow, blessing her. *'Take heart, daughter. Your faith has healed you.'*[34]

Daughter, daughter. What about my daughter?

At that moment I saw one of my attendants pushing through the crowd. He was shaking his head at me. 'It's too late,' he called. 'She's gone. Don't bother the rabbi further.'[35]

Jesus overheard him and turned to me. *'Don't be afraid. Just believe.'*[36]

And somewhere, out of some hidden corner of my heart that was still twelve-years old and still trusted heaven implicitly, I remembered a word. 'Shibboleth,' I breathed. *I make covenant with you, my king. I take your tzitzit in my hand by this word and I believe you come in the name of Yahweh Rapha.*

By the time we arrived back at my house, the flute-players, pipers and professional wailers were already there. Jesus ignored them and went in. 'Get out!' he roared at the doorway to my daughter's room. It was the tremendous full-throated growl of a lion and I was startled by its ferocity. I thought, as did everyone else, that he meant all the mourners. But I realised later he was shouting at the Rephaim, telling them to leave my child alone.

The mourners scurried out in fright. Only my anguished wife and my father in his tear-stained tallit remained, along with three of Jesus' own disciples. If it is hard for a father to outlive his child, it is harder still for a grandfather to outlive his grandchild. There was no sound coming from my father, but his body was wracked with voiceless sobs.

My daughter was lying there, her face peaceful at last, the torments of fever gone. Jesus nudged my trembling father aside and sat down on the edge of the bed. Taking off his own tallit, he lifted my daughter up and wrapped her in it like a shroud. Then he laid her back down. 'The Rephaim do not want to relinquish their hold.' He gazed at my father. 'They linger. What is the verdict that will dismiss them?'

34. Matthew 9:22 NIV

35. Mark 5:35

36. Mark 5:36 NIV

My father looked at him stupidly, as if to say, *Surely you of all people know.* He sniffed and wiped his nose, while Jesus waited. 'I don't know,' my father said finally.

Jesus said nothing. He just lifted one wing of the tallit, then the other. And he gazed again intently at my father.

'Ahh!' My father raised one finger. I saw understanding dawn on his face. He grasped the corners of his own prayer shawl and, lifting them on high, he cried in a loud voice, *'The Sun of Righteousness will rise with healing in his wings.'* And then he reached for the tzitzit on the tallit Jesus had wrapped around my daughter and again he cried, 'I say again, *"The Sun of Righteousness will rise with healing in his wings."*

I heard the howl, not in my ears this time, but in my mind as the lords of the underworld fled from the room. Jesus nodded at my father, and then bent over my daughter and breathed, 'Talitha — *little girl, little girl in the tallit —* koum, *rise!'*

Rise with the Sun of Righteousness. And she blinked, and she stirred and she looked askance at all the people in her room. And as she got up and my father bellowed with joy and hugged my laughing wife, I began to shake with violent weeping. For some joys are almost too great for the soul to bear.

This mending was almost beyond my comprehension. I saw the frayed and broken threads of past tragedies that had been woven together in a single hour: I saw the stories my father had told me on the journey through Gilead knitted back together in a seamless mending. And I saw more too: I had never realised before how deeply the loss of his mother must have affected our forefather Joseph, the patriarch of our tribe. Yet it must have done, for why would Jesus have repaired something that did not need it?

The woman on the wharf who had been cured of her bleeding had been just as much cursed as Rachel was. Both were cursed with barrenness and a bleeding unto death, Rachel quickly, the woman by slow attrition. And both had sought help from healers: the woman from doctors and Rachel from the teraphim

— she would not have stolen them otherwise. For both, it cost them all they had.

The restoration of Jesus was all knotted together with the Rephaim and Gilead in common. Rachel's tragedy began there in Gilead with her deceit over the teraphim; also from Gilead was the heartbreaking story of Jephthah's daughter, a child whose life was cut prematurely short and whose story had almost been paralleled by my daughter; and then, of course, the massacres at Jabesh Gilead and by Jephthah's men at the fords of the Jordan were also great unhealed wounds that caused us all to be wary and suspicious of one another.

No wonder I'd received word and warning about Jesus — it wasn't just that he posed a threat to power, he was a natural enemy of every tribe and clan in Israel who nurtured and cultivated, and even passionately defended the 'them-and-us' mentality that preserved our family identity. He reached across that divide between brothers, he broke open the walls that separated us and bridged the gaps, healing the past as well as the present.

He was the new foundation my father had longed for, to replace the defiled cornerstone of the Temple in Zion. Isaiah had seen the Lord, high and lifted up, with the train of his robe filling the Temple. He had seen the glory of the healing in the wings of the prayer shawl of the Lord Almighty. He had seen the hem of his garment as it brought righteousness to the Temple. With Isaiah, I could say, *'Woe to me! I am ruined! For I am a man of unclean lips, and I live among a people of unclean lips, and my eyes have seen the King, the Lord Almighty.'*[37]

How could I explain all of the wonder that engulfed me, along with the fear? For my eyes had also seen the King, the Lord Almighty.

What word could I say to Him to express my gratitude? That word, I knew, was not 'Shibboleth,' the word that speaks of holding on to his prayer shawl. It is a much harder, much simpler one.

'Lord.'

---

37. Isaiah 6:5 NIV

If you could understand a single grain of wheat, you would die of wonder.

Martin Luther

NOTES

Both Mark and Luke recount the incidents of the healing of the woman with the issue of blood and the raising of Jairus' daughter. Only Mark, however, reveals the Aramaic phrase Jesus spoke to the little girl.

Many commentaries highlight the commonalities between these two interwoven stories.

The shared elements in the lives of the woman and the girl are:

- The woman has been bleeding for 12 years; the girl is 12 years old.
- They are both, of course, female
- They are both extremely ill
- They are both unclean; one by virtue of her incessant bleeding, the other when she becomes a lifeless body

There is a fifth connection — the most significant of all — that is generally overlooked.

- Both healings are linked to the touch of Jesus's tallit.

A tallit is a fringed prayer shawl that went right around the body. The ends were called 'wings' and the long knotted strings that projected from the fringe were called 'feathers'. When Scripture speaks of 'sheltering under God's wings' or being 'covered by His feathers', it isn't actually theriomorphising Him into a bird. Rather, it's referring to the prayers He offers on our behalf as He wraps Himself in His tallit and shields us within its embrace.

The 'barrenness' of both the woman and the girl in these gospel accounts recall the five barren women in the Hebrew portion of the Scriptures who eventually give birth:

- Sarah
- Rebekah
- Rachel
- Hannah
- the wife of Manoah[38]

38.
The mother of Samson.

Only the narrative involving Rachel alludes to bleeding, so her story is the natural place to look for further links to the past. The particular incident in question occurs when she is hiding her father's teraphim by sitting on them. He is searching for these household gods and she asks him to excuse her from standing, claiming that she is menstruating.

There are several levels of dishonour in her statement but the immediately significant one is the violation of the spiritual principle to not dishonour any of God's creation. This tenet includes fallen angels and other ungodly beings. We can ask God to rebuke such unholy entities — that is, to return honour in due measure — but we cannot disrespect, revile, insult or disparage without retaliation.

Rachel was doubly cursed: once at her own hands by deliberately scheming to steal her father's household gods, *the spirit-healers*; and once inadvertently by her husband when he called down death upon the thief. Perhaps that is why Jesus is involved in two healings: because of the double curse.

Her deception took place in a land claimed by spirit beings called Rephaim — *ancestral ghost warriors* said to command, among other things, the power of healing. The word 'teraphim' is related to Rephaim, so she was humiliating them in their own territory where their power was at a maximum.

It is the Rephaim, *the spirit-healers,* that Jesus opposed that day in Capernaum,[39] a town on the shore of the Sea of Galilee. Its history prior to the time He established it as His ministry base is unknown. But in its recent past, just before Jesus made it His home, a centurion funded the local synagogue. As a result, the town elders were prompted to support this Roman soldier when he wanted help from Jesus. Naturally the centurion — whom I've named Antonius, though Scripture doesn't identify him — would have known Jairus, the synagogue leader. The circumstances, however, were probably different from my portrayal of them. I've entirely invented Antonius' excuse to stand in the synagogue each week. I have not, however, invented his motivation to learn about the Jewish faith.

Jairus is identified in Mark's gospel as well as Luke's. His name is therefore the *only* clue we have within the text to be able to track back into history and learn what restoration Jesus accomplished through this double healing event — and be sure it's a matter that goes back to the duplicity of Rachel.

The name Jairus comes from Jair, *he enlightens*. Jair was the son of Manasseh, the son of Joseph. He was therefore the great-grandson of Jacob and Rachel — fourth generation from the

39.
Capernaum means *the village of Nahum* or *village of comfort*, and can also be translated *threshold of Nahum, threshold of comfort, cornerstone of Nahum, cornerstone of comfort*.

patriarch and matriarch of all Israel. He was called Jair of Gilead. He was famous for conquering the towns of Bashan — the land of King Og, last of the Rephaim — and renaming them Havvoth Jair, *villages of Jair,* after himself.

His connection to Rachel is more than ancestral. It is also geographical.

Gilead, *camel hump*, Bashan, *serpent*, and Argob, *heaps of rock*, were in the same general area east of the Jordan. The confrontation between Jacob and his uncle Laban occurred here. Jacob had secretly upped and left the land where he'd been living for the past 22 years. He'd taken his flocks, herds, wives, sons and daughter and cut loose from his uncle's domination and manipulation. Laban had followed the fleeing household and caught up with them somewhere in Gilead. Warned in a dream, he kept his cool and restrained his aggression, expressed his sorrow that Jacob had taken off without giving him a chance to farewell his daughters and grandchildren, then demanded his teraphim back.

Now 'teraphim' is usually translated *household gods*. Their purpose is unclear, their function is uncertain — we can only surmise that they were figurines from the fact Rachel was able to hide them in a camel pack and sit on top of them. The derivation of their name, 'teraphim', does help a little — it comes from 'rephaim', *spirits, shades* or *ghosts*, from 'rapha', *spirit, ghost, giant, heal, cure.*

It does not seem in any way coincidental that in the land of the Rephaim[40] that the contentious issue between Jacob and Laban was the teraphim: household gods in some way related to the Rephaim. Nor does it seem coincidental that this would become Gilead, probably from Galeed, *witness heap*, the name Jacob gave to the pile of stones that must have looked like a *camel's hum*p and that was to *watch over* the pledges Jacob and Laban had made to one another.

CG Jung said, 'The gods have become our diseases.' It seems a dramatic and bizarre statement, yet it recognises our deep complicity with the enemy. Instead of covenantal loyalty to Jesus, we have alliances that allow us to be afflicted. When Jesus healed the people who came to Him, they knew He was not only treating physical disease but the demonic affliction behind it. They understood demons to be the spirits of part-human, part-angel hybrids. The bodies of these demons had once been giants, like those who were drowned in the flood of Noah. But their spirits lived on, craving re-embodiment and looking for access to living flesh — preferably to take over and possess human consciousness.

40.
It was still the territory of the Rephaim in the time of Jacob and would be so for another five centuries until the Israelites under Moses and Joshua defeated Og, the last of the Rephaim.

41.
This duality of thought is also expressed in the 'serpent staff' that, even today, still symbolises the profession of healing. The venom of the serpent can be fatal; antivenin produced from the same venom can cure.

We can catch a small glimpse of the conflict over the centuries about the nature of disease: for some people, the Rephaim were the *spirit healers*; for others, the Rephaim were the disease inflicters.[41]

Back in the time of Jacob and Laban, the Rephaim still had a reputation for curing disease. They were considered denizens of the underworld and were, in the time of Moses, Joshua and Jair, ruled by King Og. Assuming Og's iron bed was an accurate indication of his size,[42] he was well over four metres tall. However his bed may not be true to his height. It happens to be exactly the same dimensions as the sacred marriage bed in the temple of the Babylonian deity Marduk,[43] so it may simply be constructed to a ritual pattern.

The region ruled by Og, then called Bashan, *land of the serpent* or *land of the dragon*, now extends from the Golan Heights in northern Israel through into Syria. It is bounded in the north by Mount Hermon and the Anti-Lebanon Range. Thousands of dolmens — upright stones topped by massive slab lintels that form the entrance to underground passages — are still scattered across the region. In addition, the labyrinthine stone structure dubbed here by me as 'Og's sun temple' still exists as an eerie landscape feature not far from the ruins of Gamla, the fortress city perched on a hill shaped like a camel's hump. It is now called Gilgal Refaim — or Rujm el-Hiri or Rogem Hiri — *wheel of spirits*, and is close by the Nahal Daliyot stream. Just north of it is a ridge, shaped like a serpent, and dotted with tombs.[44]

Further in the same direction is triple-peaked Mount Hermon, the highest mountain in both Syria and Israel. The borders of Lebanon, Syria and Israel meet there. Hermon, *accursed*, is named for the group of fallen angels who, according to the Book of Enoch, descended to its summit and there pledged, with mutual oaths and anathemas, to both seek human women as wives and share any divine punishment that followed. These angels went on to father the giants, who in turn fathered the 'mighty men of old' — demi-gods and monsters whose bodies were destroyed in the Flood but whose spirits lived on as demons.

Now it wasn't just the Israelites who considered the land of Bashan to be the haunt of giants, monsters and ghosts. The Mesopotamian *Epic of Gilgamesh* attests to the belief that the cedar forests of the nearby mountain ranges were inhabited and guarded by Humbaba, an ogre, monster or giant, whose name is related to *lizard*.

42.
9 cubits by 4 cubits: see Deuteronomy 3:11

43.
thetorah.com/article/og-king-of-bashan-underworld-ruler-or-ancient-giant (accessed 2 May 2023)

44.
An altitude photo of this 'serpent mound' shown with Gilgal Refaim can be found at derekpgilbert.com/2021/12/29/the-second-coming-of-saturn-part-13-bashan-land-of-the-serpent/ (accessed 2 May 2023).

Bashan, as the *land of the serpent* and also the land of the Rephaim, *healers*, reminds us of the serpent as a traditional healing symbol. Today we often see the symbol of two entwined snakes around a winged staff as an emblem for some branch of the medical profession. Originally, it was one snake spiralling around a rod, without wings, and was called the 'asklepion'.

This is the matrix of ideas that we need to be just a little familiar with so that we can extract the nature of the healing of history that Jesus was undertaking that day in Capernaum. From the story of the woman who had spent all her money on doctors to no avail, we can see the emergence of the motif of the healers. From her continual bleeding, we know we have to look for a woman who was afflicted by blood loss. From her desire to touch the hem of Jesus' garment, we know she understood the significance of that action and that she had most likely travelled in from east of the Jordan. The only other time we hear of people desperate to touch the edge of His mantle was in Gennesaret[45] where everyone was healed.[46] This region was south of Capernaum, on the Sea of Galilee. It was on the opposite shore to old Gilead where Jair had his thirty towns.

Gilead should attune us to a *camel's hump*, and to Galeed, *witness heap*. That in turn should remind us of Rachel sitting there right next to the cairn named Galeed, perched on a camel's pack and hiding the 'teraphim' in the baggage underneath her, all the while claiming to be bleeding.

The hills of Gilead also marked, in later times, the countryside where Jephthah's daughter spent two months with her friends, mourning. She would have been about 12 years old. And it was across this terrain that the men of Ephraim fled after they tried to gas-light Jephthah and claim he had not sent to them in his call for war. They had already abandoned the covenant binding the tribal brotherhood together when they refused to respond to Jephthah's muster. Yet, when the men of Gilead gave them a simple way back — a gentle reminder of who they really should be, defenders of the covenant not transgressors of it — they couldn't take it.

Chaim Bentorah makes the point that it's highly unlikely 42,000 men came up to the fords of the Jordan one by one.[47] The 'password' should quickly have passed back from the survivors of one group to the next, along with the stern admonition: practise the *shhh* sound.

The fact that this didn't happen, the fact that the men of Ephraim continued to say a word with overtones that demanded servitude and subservience, hints that they were so deep in 'enemy mode' that they chose to die rather than sacrifice the sense of superiority that had become

---

45. Mark 6:53

46. Mark 6:56

47. Chaim Bentorah, *Time Loop: Seeing America's Future in Persia's Past*, True Potential Inc 2020. This book also explains the difference in derivation of *sibboleth* and *shibboleth* and thus the background nuances in the words that go far beyond mere accent and local dialect.

integral to their clan identity. They would not lower themselves to become equal with the ruffians and outlaws of Gilead. Perhaps the incident is an example of group narcissism — since narcissism results from an inability to process shame. It's possible they were so ashamed of not rallying to Jephthah's call, the lies and threats were a natural outcome of the burden of shame they were still carrying.

Certainly we can see shame playing a huge role in the story of Jesus and the woman with the issue of blood. And there would have been shame — or at least there was the pretence of shame — in Rachel's interaction with her father where she used bleeding to conceal theft and dishonour. Because whether she was telling the truth or not about her menstrual condition, there couldn't have been many things more dishonourable in that culture than parking yourself on top of figurines that allegedly housed the spirits of your ancestors.

It's unwise to dishonour anyone, but extraordinarily unwise to dishonour spirits. Both Peter and Jude in their epistles testify to this principle. Jude outlines the care we should take:

> *'Ungodly people pollute their own bodies, reject authority and heap abuse on celestial beings. But even the archangel Michael, when he was disputing with the devil about the body of Moses, did not himself dare to condemn him for slander but said, "The Lord rebuke you!"'*
>
> Jude 1:8–9 NIV

This quotation concerning the archangel Michael and the devil is from a document called *The Testament of Moses,* or *The Assumption of Moses.*

Rachel dishonoured the Rephaim in their own territory. She covenanted with them through taking into her possession the statues that housed them, even while subjecting them to immense disrespect by squatting on top of them. In fact, she dishonoured many more than the Rephaim — she dishonoured her father, her brothers who would rightfully inherit the teraphim, her husband, and God Himself. She set herself up for massive spiritual retaliation.

If we do the calculations based on the time Jacob spent with Laban, taking out the seven years he worked for Rachel's hand and then the various pregnancies of his other wives before Rachel finally conceived, then her death probably occurred when Joseph was five years old. It would have been a devastating loss for such a young child.

I have a theory that parents tend to name their children for the unresolved trauma of their family line, prophesying every time they call out to them by name: 'It's your destiny to heal this problem that has afflicted our family for generations.' Joseph's mother died at Ephrath, near Bethlehem. He named his younger son, Ephraim, a constant reminder of that place. But the name was also prophetic of Ephraim's destiny to bind up the tragedy of his grandmother's death as well as all that led to it and all that followed after. Because it was the grief of losing Rachel that caused Jacob to so favour Joseph that his brothers hated him. And assuming Joseph was indeed five when Rachel passed away, then it was twelve years later — again the portentous number twelve — that his brothers sold him into slavery.

The complex history of this healing starts with Rachel, passes down to Joseph and then to his sons, Manasseh and Ephraim. Manasseh is an ancestor of Jair, Gilead and also Jephthah. And in the story of the men of Ephraim attacking Jephthah, we see the descendants of these two brothers at each others' throats.

So the issue of healing throughout the history of these tribes was inextricably bound up with covenant loyalty. That is made evident in the backstory, yet it's also made clear in the desire of so many diseased people to touch the hem of Jesus' prayer shawl.

Quite a few commentators say that, 'Talitha, koum,' the words Jesus speaks to the 12-year-old child have very tender overtones, not simply of *little girl* but of *little lamb*. Others suggest that He doesn't merely say, 'Little girl, arise!' but 'Little girl in the tallit, arise!' And still others point out that this is technically and linguistically impossible.

But Jesus is a poet. Words bow before Him. As the Word made flesh, He can be as playful as He likes with different verbal nuances. He doesn't need to confine Himself to the technical constraints of linguistic theory. 'We are God's poetry,' says Ephesians 2:10, though most translations opt for *masterpiece*, *workmanship* or *handiwork* instead of the more literal *poetry*. Another verse that tells us Jesus is a poet is the very last verse of John's gospel:

> *Jesus **did** many other things as well. If every one of them were written down, I suppose that even the whole world would not have room for the books that would be written.*
>
> John 21:25 NIV

That emphasised word, *did*, actually describes *making poetry*. It's an exceptionally lovely mirror for the opening verse of John's gospel: the beginning is about the Word, the ending about the making of poetry.

The presence of the tallit would be such an enormously significant link between both stories I find it difficult to believe it is absent in the story of Jairus' daughter.

Her grandfather is not present in either of the biblical accounts. I made him up, I admit, because I wanted a character to unequivocally declare allegiance to the Sun of Righteousness as foretold by the prophet Malachi who spoke of a day when those who fear God's name would go out, leaping like calves because the Sun of Righteousness had arisen with healing in His wings.

And that's why people wanted to touch the wings of Jesus' tallit — because they wanted to unite themselves with His prayer life, to be at one with Him, in union with Him, in covenantal oneness with Him, as their heavenly mediator.

Isaiah's vision of the Lord, high and lifted up, with the train of His robe filling the Temple is a vision of healing for the nation. It happened in the year that King Uzziah died — and, in essence, the vision reverses the tragic defilement Uzziah had brought upon the kingdom through his attempt to usurp the role of the priests. Uzziah had invaded the sanctuary and, taking coals from the altar of incense, was about to offer prayer to God when he was struck with leprosy. From that point on, the prayer life of the nation must have been contaminated because Isaiah's vision involves a seraph reversing Uzziah's action by taking a coal from the heavenly altar of incense and placing it on Isaiah's lips. This would purify the uncleanness of his words and prayers, as well as those of the people.

Yet the train of the Lord's robe filling the Temple shows us His prayer shawl alone brings healing to the nation, not any sacrificial offerings. Uzziah's foreign policy is implicitly condemned in Isaiah description. We know, from archaeological evidence, that Uzziah had close ties with Assyria during the height of its power. Now the train of the robe of the Assyrian king grew ever longer as his victories increased.[48] He'd attach the ceremonial robes of the kings he'd conquered to his own so that, when he entered his local temple, the train would flow out behind him as a visual statement to his triumphs.

When Isaiah spoke the train of the Lord's robe *filling* the Temple, he was reminding his own people that God's prayer shawl was so long He ruled all the earth. The empire conquered by the armies of Assyria could hardly be compared with the kingdom of heaven and the sovereignty of the Lord of Hosts — the Lord of Angel Armies.

---

48. See: chaimbentorah.com/2021/03/hebrew-word-study-train-shul/ (accessed 27 April 2023)

Yet the fact the Lord's garment was a tallit indicated that prayer itself had become so tainted that God Himself had to intervene to purify it. He had to bring healing even to the nature of intercession!

It's the same issue for us today. Our bodies are temples of the Holy Spirit. But have we allowed the train of the Lord's robe to fill us and purify us? Or have we, like Uzziah, decided that the only way prayer can be done right is if we do it ourselves? Do we invite Jesus to be our mediator or do we go our own way?

Healing is found through the prayers of Jesus, our advocate, as He mediates for us in heaven. But we must be in covenantal oneness for that to take effect. All too often we assume we have no problems in that arena when, in fact, we are deeply complicit with some spirit like, but not necessarily identical to, the Rephaim. We cannot be truly one with Yahweh Rapha if we have agreements with the Rephaim. We cannot be truly one with the Resurrection and the Life if we have a covenant with Death. We cannot be truly one with the Light of the World[49] if we have not renounced our allegiance to Darkness.

We think we're fine because we've never heard of the Rephaim before, so how could we possibly have a partnership with them? Or a covenant with Death — it's an unthinkable idea because, when it comes right down to it, we have no clue about how to raise a covenant. As for a pact with Darkness, no way — always steered clear of stuff like that. This is a complete misunderstanding of the nature of covenant and its associated vows: covenant is not simply an especially solemn contract. Its essential character is the oneness that is created. The obligations, responsibilities, blessings and curses do not cease to exist when the parties who pledged them in the first place die. A covenantal agreement passes down family lines until someone recognises its ungodly nature and decides to revoke it. But that person, realising that various curses will be triggered by a retraction — and indeed may already be unleashed — needs to present the covenant to Jesus and ask Him to annul it through the power of His cross.

He longs to activate the finished work of His atonement on our behalf. But He doesn't treat its operation as a default switching mechanism. We'd bypass relationship if it was.

Jesus doesn't just want to heal us as individuals. He wants to heal our families and our communities. He wants us to take hold, by faith, of the tzitzit on the wings of His tallit. He wants us to renounce our alliances with the enemy, and covenant with Him instead. He wants us to unite our mustard-seed of belief in Him with His boundless infinity of faith, so we can be whole in His name.

48.
Even if we are in covenant with the 'Light of the World', we need to check our assumptions. If our ancestors have cut a covenant with Mithras, the so-called 'Light of the World' defeated by Jesus, then if it has never been revoked, it would almost certainly still be operational.

THE NATION OF ISRAEL AND THE TALLIT

In central Jerusalem, on Ben Yehuda Street, is a pedestrian mall filled with cafés, shops and street vendors. It is named after Eliezer Ben Yehuda who was responsible for reviving Hebrew as a modern language. As visitors approach the mall, there is a clocktower inscribed with the words *Tallitha Kumi*.

The Tower commemorates the rebirth of Israel as a nation after nearly two thousand years. During those two millennia Israel appeared as if dead, just like the little girl on the verge of womanhood who had fallen asleep and who needed a visitation from God to wake her up. The words, *Tallitha Kumi*, mean *'Little girl, get up!'* so they are appropriate for the arising of Israel as a modern nation.

However the words also mean: *'Little girl who is wrapped in the tallit, get up!'* This too is appropriate since the flag of Israel is modelled on the tallit. The two blue stripes symbolise the Sovereignty of God, while the six-pointed star in the middle, the Shield of David, is a reminder of the great Messianic hope of redemption.

Because the tallit is a prayer shawl and a reminder of God's faithfulness to His people, so then the flag of modern Israel incorporates prayer in its design. Whenever it is displayed, it messages to the nation and to the world at large that our sovereign God, the Lord Almighty, is constant and compassionate and moreover is able to bring life out of death.

> *Thrones were put in place,*
> *and the Ancient of Days was seated;*
> *His garment was white as snow,*
> *and the hair of His head was like pure wool.*
> *His throne was a fiery flame,*
> *its wheels a burning fire.*

Daniel 7:9 NKJV

Based on this passage from the prophecy of Daniel, where the clothing of God is described as being *'white as snow'*, along with Isaiah's vision of the train of the Lord's robe filling the temple, it was thought that God wrapped Himself in a tallit.

The tallit was also a symbol of holiness—that is, being set apart for a special purpose. The 'tzitzit', the knotted fringe of the garment, were considered to be like feathers on the wings of the shawl. They were made of linen and wool, a mixture that was only allowed to priests. Thus the tallit is a symbol to remind the people that they are a holy priesthood, a people set apart out of all the nations for the Lord's own.

> *When the Most High assigned lands to the nations,*
> *when He divided up the human race,*
> *He established the boundaries of the peoples*
> *according to the number in His heavenly court.*
> *For the people of Israel belong to the Lord;*
> *Jacob is His special possession.*

Deuteronomy 32:8–9 NLT

The people of Israel as well as those who have been spiritually grafted in can shelter under the wings of God's prayer shawl. But, as a royal priesthood, we are also called to prayer on behalf of all nations. In the last century, we have seen the nation of Israel revived, just as the little girl wrapped in the tallit was. That rebirth is the fulfilment of the promises of God pledged in His Word, and a reminder to us that He remains always faithful and will surely keep His personal promises to us too.

Discussion Questions:

(1) When people drop into what is called 'enemy mode', they will kill to protect their identities. Others are willing to die to protect their identities. In what ways can pride in our own individual identity or group identity get in the way of survival, recovery or healing?

(2) What are some common emotional, mental and spiritual hindrances to healing?

(3) The people who sought to touch the hem of His garment were not simply asking Jesus to be their Saviour and heal them, they were also surrendering to Him as Lord and King in an expression of covenant loyalty. What is the difference between asking Jesus to be our Saviour and asking Him to be our Lord?

Ben Yehuda Street Mall

Prayer

Heavenly Father, holy, holy, holy is Your Name.

With Your angel hosts, I proclaim, 'Holy, holy, holy.'

Lord God Almighty, Isaiah saw in a vision the train of Your robe filling the temple. The wings of Your prayer shawl, the fringe of Your mantle, the hem of Your garment — he witnessed it descending to cleanse, to heal, to purify, and to lift out defilement and dishonour brought in by a king who believed that, if you wanted something done right, especially in prayer, you have to do it yourself.

But that's untrue, Lord. If you want something done right, especially in prayer, it's a matter for Your Son, Jesus, the perfect mediator and advocate.

Lord and Father, my body is the temple of the Holy Spirit. But like that king in the time of Isaiah, I don't honour You or trust You as is truly right or righteous. Forgive me, Father, and fill me — fill me as Your temple with the train of the robe of Jesus, the Lord Almighty. Let the fringe of His prayer shawl ripple through me as grain bends in the field, submitting to the wind. Let me bow to the breeze of Your Holy Spirit, let me catch the edge of Your garment to covenant with You and be made whole — body and soul.

I ask You to make me one with You, covenantally one.

I ask You to make me one with Your Son, covenantally one.

I ask You to make me one with Your Holy Spirit, covenantally one.

I ask You to make me one with You, Three-in-One, covenantally one.

I ask Jesus to carry this petition to You through the mediating flow of His prayers. Thank You for Your favour, Your love and Your endless world-healing grace.

In the name of Jesus of Nazareth. Amen

Acknowledgments & Attributions

Photo and Art Credits

Front cover and page 4 – to_csa / iStock | Description: Poppy field

Page 7 – Francis ODonohue / iStock | Description: High angle view of Sea of Galilee and Beatitudes fields

Page 8 – lucidwaters / Canstock

Page 10 – svarshik1 / Depositphotos | Description: Remains of buildings and stone walls on the ruins of the Gamla city, Golan Heights

Page 11 – hildr / iStock | Description: Dolmens in Gamla Reserve

Page 12 – svarshik / iStock | Description: The remnants of the megalithic complex of the early Bronze Age – Wheels of Spirits – Rujum Al-Hiri – Gilgal Rephaeem – on the Golan Heights in Israel

Page 15 – johannes86/ iStock| Description: Ancient ruins of amphitheatre in Beit Shean National Park, Israel

Page 16 – Eyal Granith / Dreamstime | Description: Jewish men praying in a synagogue with Tallit

Page 18 – DesignPicsInc / Depositphotos | Description: Young Jesus and High Priest

Page 19 – Zev Radovan / Alamy | Description: Rachel had stolen the images of the Teraphim that were her father's

Page 21 – iloveotto / Canstock | Description: Asia style textures and backgrounds

Page 22 – Juli Kosolapova / Unsplash | Description: Wadi Rum, Aqaba, Jordan

Page 25 – Todd Bolen / BiblePlaces.com | Description: Jabesh Gilead, Tell Maqlub, summit with flowers

Page 26 – alexeys / Depositphotos | Description: Beit She'an || Greg Rosenke / Unsplash | Description: raven

Page 27 – Own Work / Wikimedia | Description: Pistacia palaestina, terebinth || leandro fregoni / Unsplash | Description: work bee

Page 29 – Gioele Fazzeri / Unsplash | Description: Portrait of a medieval warrior

Page 30 – Igor Strukov / Depositphotos | Description: Wheat in Sunset.

Page 32 – Eyal Granith / Dreamstime | Description: Jewish man praying in a synagogue with Tallit

Page 33/34 – RnDmS / iStock | Description: Sunrise view of the Sea of Galilee

Page 37 – Jacek_Sopotnicki / iStock | Description: Synagogue in Jesus Town of Capernaum

Page 39 – PhotoGranary / Lightstock | Description: Portrait of the biblical carpenter Joseph in his workshop

Page 41 – fxquadro / Depositphotos | Description: Imperial soldier holding helmet and short sword

Page 42 – DCPmedia / Lightstock | Christ walking slowly covered with a tallit in a beautiful poppies field at sunset

Page 43 – LUMO-The Gospels for the visual age / Lightstock | Description: Jesus walking amongst a crowd

Page 45 – LUMO-The Gospels for the visual age / Lightstock | Description: Jairus's daughter

Page 47 – Yehoshua Halevi / iStock | Description: A hand gathers and holds the tzitzit, strings tied to the four corners of a tallit or Jewish prayer shawl

Page 51 – LUMO-The Gospels for the visual age / Lightstock | Description: Jairus's daughter

Pages 52/53 – Bas van den Eijkhof / Lightstock | Description: Jewel studded crown in a field of wheat

Pages 56/57 (background) – svarshik / iStock | Description: The remnants of the megalithic complex of the early Bronze Age – Wheels of Spirits – Rujum Al-Hiri – Gilgal Rephaeem – on the Golan Heights in Israel

Pages 58/59 (background) – alefbet / Depositphotos | Description: Gamla Nature Reserve, Israel

Page 65 – Eitan Simanor / Alamy | Description: Jerusalem. Ben Yehuda pedestrian street.

Page 67 – Beckon Creative | Description: Tzitzit

Design, including endpapers and iconography: Beckon Creative | beckoncreative.biz

Bible Versions

Scripture quotations marked CEV are from the Contemporary English Version Copyright © 1991, 1992, 1995 by American Bible Society. Used by Permission.

Scripture quotations marked ESV are taken from the ESV® Bible (The Holy Bible, English Standard Version®), copyright © 2001 by Crossway, a publishing ministry of Good News Publishers. Used by permission. All rights reserved.

Scripture quotations marked ISV are taken from the Holy Bible: International Standard Version®. Copyright © 1996-forever by The ISV Foundation. ALL RIGHTS RESERVED INTERNATIONALLY. Used by permission.

Scripture quotations marked NIV are taken from the Holy Bible, New International Version®, NIV®. Copyright © 1973, 1978, 1984, 2011 by Biblica, Inc.™ Used by permission of Zondervan. All rights reserved worldwide. www.zondervan.com The "NIV" and "New International Version" are trademarks registered in the United States Patent and Trademark Office by Biblica, Inc.™.

Scripture quotations marked NKJV are taken from the New King James Version. Copyright © 1982 by Thomas Nelson, Inc. Used by permission. All rights reserved.

Scripture quotations marked NLT are taken from the Holy Bible, New Living Translation, copyright 1996, 2004. Used by permission of Tyndale House Publishers, Inc., Wheaton, Illinois 60189. All rights reserved.

© Anne Hamilton 2023

Published by Armour Books

P. O. Box 492, Corinda QLD 4075 AUSTRALIA

ISBN: 978-1-925380-69-9

All rights reserved. No part of this publication may be reproduced, stored in, or introduced into a retrieval system, or transmitted, in any form, or by any means (electronic, mechanical, photocopying, recording or otherwise) without the prior written permission of the publisher.

A catalogue record for this book is available from the National Library of Australia

O Sabbath rest by Galilee,
O calm of hills above,
where Jesus knelt to share with Thee
the silence of eternity,
interpreted by love!

Drop Thy still dews of quietness,
till all our strivings cease;
take from our souls the strain and stress,
and let our ordered lives confess
the beauty of Thy peace.

Breathe through the heats of our desire
Thy coolness and Thy balm;
let sense be dumb, let flesh retire;
speak through the earthquake, wind, and fire,
O still, small voice of calm!

John Greenleaf Whittier

www.ingramcontent.com/pod-product-compliance
Lightning Source LLC
Chambersburg PA
CBHW050750110526
44591CB00002B/37